WAR MACHINES

COMBAT HELICOPTERS

by
David West

CRABTREE

PUBLISHING COMPANY
WWW.CRABTREEBOOKS.COM

CRABTREE
PUBLISHING COMPANY
WWW.CRABTREEBOOKS.COM

Author and designer: David West

Illustrator: David West

Editorial director: Kathy Middleton

Editor: Ellen Rodger

Proofreader: Melissa Boyce

**Production coordinator
and Prepress technician**: Ken Wright

Print coordinator: Katherine Berti

Library and Archives Canada Cataloguing in Publication

Title: Combat helicopters / David West.
Names: West, David, 1956- author.
Description: Series statement: War machines | Includes index.
Identifiers: Canadiana (print) 20190099321 |
  Canadiana (ebook) 20190099348 |
  ISBN 9780778766797 (softcover) |
  ISBN 9780778766650 (hardcover) |
  ISBN 9781427124074 (HTML)
Subjects: LCSH: Military helicopters—Juvenile literature.
Classification: LCC UG1230 .W47 2019 |
  DDC j358.4/183—dc23

Library of Congress Cataloging-in-Publication Data

Names: West, David, 1956- author.
Title: Combat helicopters / David West.
Description: New York : Crabtree Publishing Company, [2019]
  | Series: War machines | Includes index. |
  Audience: Grades 7-8. | Audience: Ages 10-14 and up. |
Identifiers: LCCN 2019014225 (print) |
  LCCN 2019017525 (ebook) |
  ISBN 9781427124074 (Electronic) |
  ISBN 9780778766650 (hardcover) |
  ISBN 9780778766797 (pbk.)
Subjects: LCSH: Military helicopters--Juvenile literature.
Classification: LCC UG1230 (ebook) |
  LCC UG1230 .W45 2019 (print) | DDC 358.4/183--dc23
LC record available at https://lccn.loc.gov/2019014225

Crabtree Publishing Company
www.crabtreebooks.com   1-800-387-7650

Printed in the U.S.A./072019/CG20190501

Published by Crabtree Publishing Company in 2020

**Published in Canada
Crabtree Publishing**
616 Welland Ave.
St. Catharines, ON
L2M 5V6

**Published in the United States
Crabtree Publishing**
PMB 59051, 350 Fifth Ave.
59th Floor,
New York, NY

Contents

...ed in

Korean

...ounded

...als. It wasn't

...t helicopters

...s conflict,

...s. They

...e were

Today, military forces use helicopters for multiple roles, including traditional observation and targeting. They are important for quick troop transport and medical evacuation (medevac). Helicopters also provide **close air support** (CAS) by attacking enemy troops. They are even important in antisubmarine warfare. Military technology has become so advanced that drone helicopters are now standard for observation as well as bombing missions.

Rotating Blades

In 1923, Spanish engineer Juan de la Cierva built a new type of aircraft. It was powered by a propeller and had similar controls to an airplane. Instead of wings, it had rotating blades to provide lift. The new invention was called an autogyro.

Autogyros, or gyrocopters, are not the same as helicopters because the engine does not power the rotors. In the event of engine failure, autogyros can land safely. As long as forward momentum is maintained,

A British Royal Air Force Avro Rota autogyro (1) flies close to the south coast of England during the Battle of Britain to check the range of coastal radar stations. A pair of Spitfires (2) patrol in the background.

the rotors will keep spinning to provide lift. Gyrocopters had limited use during World War II (WWII). A military version of the Cierva C.30, the Avro 671 Rota, was used by the Royal Air Force (RAF) during the **Battle of Britain** (July 10 to October 31, 1940). The Imperial Japanese Army developed the Kayaba Ka-1 autogyro for **reconnaissance** flights. It also armed some with small **depth charges** for antisubmarine warfare.

The Russians produced an armed autogyro, Kamov A7–3A. It flew successful night operations in 1942.

The First Helicopters

The first operational helicopters were being built by
1936. Some helicopter designs were in limited
production, but it was 1942 before a helicopter with a
main rotor and tail rotor reached full-scale production.
It was designed by helicopter pioneer Igor Sikorsky.

The Sikorsky R-4 Hoverfly was mainly used by the United States for
rescues in Burma and China during WWII. Anton Flettner of Germany
produced a helicopter which had two side-by-side rotors. The design

An Fl 282 Kolibri (Hummingbird) helicopter takes off to provide artillery spotting and observation for a unit of German Nebelwerfer multiple rocket launchers during WWII.

made sure the blades of the rotors did not smack into each other. This was called an intermeshing rotor helicopter. Just 24 machines were made before the German factory was destroyed by **Allied** bombing raids. The surviving Fl 282s were used as artillery spotters, but most were shot down by **Soviet** fighters and antiaircraft fire.

The Focke-Achgelis Fa 223 Drache (Dragon) was developed in Germany during WWII. They were speedy craft, reaching 113 miles per hour (182 kph). Most were used to transport troops to mountain regions and to recover crashed aircraft.

9

It was not until the Korean War that the helicopter truly proved its usefulness in battle. U.S. general Edward A. Craig used a helicopter to see the landscape where his troops were to fight. Commanders of small units soon followed his example.

One of the major uses for helicopters during the Korean War was to ferry wounded soldiers from the front line to field hospitals. The Bell H-13 Sioux helicopter was made famous by the television show *M*A*S*H*.

U.S. infantry carry a wounded soldier to a Bell H-13 Sioux helicopter equipped with medevac panniers during the Battle of Chosin Reservoir in 1950.

It was used as an air ambulance during the war. The Sioux could carry two injured soldiers in medevac **panniers**, one on each skid. An acrylic shield protected the injured from wind. The Sikorsky H-5 also carried casualties to **MASH** units.

The Sikorsky H-5 was one of the first helicopters to see action in the Korean War. It was used to evacuate the wounded from the front line. It also ferried supplies, but was most famous for rescuing pilots behind enemy lines.

The Vietnam War saw the first large-scale use of helicopters in a combat role. The introduction of air cavalry completely changed the way war was fought. Air cavalry were troops of soldiers that could be carried swiftly by helicopters to any part of the battlefield.

The Bell UH-1 Iroquois, nicknamed "Huey," became the workhorse of the air cavalry. It also had many other roles, such as cargo transport, search and rescue, medevac, observation, and ground support.

A Bell UH-1 Iroquois from the 7th Cavalry Regiment carries troops to the landing site at the foot of the Chu Pong Massif in the Central Highlands of Vietnam. This is where the Battle of Ia Drang was fought on November 14–16, 1965.

An Air Cavalry Troop (ACT) Huey contained a platoon of six to eight troops and a door gunner. These were known as "slicks" because there were no weapon pods on the sides. Three ACTs were usually accompanied by eight or nine Bell UH-1 gunship helicopters and a number of Hughes OH-6 light observation helicopters.

The Bell UH-1N Twin Huey replaced the single-engined UH-1 in 1970. It could carry 14 passengers, along with miniguns or 40 mm grenade launchers and rocket pods.

Transport helicopters are used for carrying troops, equipment, and cargo during military operations. Some of the larger, more powerful helicopters, like the CH-47 Chinook, are capable of airlifting large loads such as artillery guns and even tanks.

The Ch-47 Chinook has twin rotors powered by two turboshaft engines. The rotors revolve in opposite directions to keep the helicopter stable. It has a rear ramp for loading cargo and three hooks underneath that can

During Operation Masher in 1966, several Boeing CH-47 Chinooks airlift artillery to mountain positions that are inaccessible by other means.

carry underslung loads. Developed during the 1960s, the Chinook is one of the few helicopters of that time still in service. It has seen action in wars from Vietnam to Afghanistan. It has also been used as a gunship armed with machine guns and rockets.

The single main-rotored Sikorsky CH-53 Sea Stallion can carry up to 55 troops in its hold. Here, it loads a Wiesel Armored Weapons Carrier. The loading ramp is in the rear.

With its growing involvement in Vietnam, the U.S. Army identified the need for an attack helicopter to replace the Bell UH-1 gunship. The Bell AH-1 Cobra became the army's first dedicated attack helicopter. It was deployed in Vietnam in 1967.

Bell AH-1 Cobras provided fire support for ground forces. They also took over the role of gunship in air cavalry regiments. Cobras formed aerial rocket artillery (ARA) battalions and "hunter-killer" teams along

A Hughes OH-6 Cayuse scout helicopter flies slow and low. This draws enemy fire and reveals the enemy's position. A Bell AH-1 Cobra then strikes with missiles and fires its chin-mounted minigun at the revealed enemy.

with OH-6A scout helicopters. The Cobra's pilot and gunner sat in tandem, or one behind the other. This made the helicopter appear slimmer, making it a more difficult target for enemy gunfire. The Cobra's awesome firepower included a 40 mm chin-mounted automatic grenade launcher, as well as wing-mounted rocket and missile launchers.

The Sikorsky CH-34 Choctaw was a multipurpose helicopter. They were called Stingers because they were armed with two machine guns and two rocket pods.

The success of gunships and attack helicopters used by the U.S. Army during the Vietnam War inspired the Soviet helicopter designer Mikhail Leont'yevich Mil. He proposed a design for a helicopter that could perform both fire support and infantry transport.

The Mil Mi-24 entered service in 1972. The five-blade main rotor and three-blade tail rotor are driven by two top-mounted turboshaft engines. The pilot and gunner share a cockpit with a "double bubble"

Three heavily armed Soviet Mil Mi-24 gunships hug the landscape as they head for their targets during the Soviet-Afghan War. Their thick armament and ability to resist enemy fire earned them the nickname "flying tanks."

canopy in front of the fuselage. The Mil MI-24 can carry eight troops. Its titanium rotors and heavily armored fuselage resist impacts from 12.7 mm rounds. On its wing pods, it can carry a variety of missiles, rockets, and bombs. The Mi-24 first saw combat during the **Soviet-Afghan War**.

Mi-24 pilots did not like the extra weight of troops, so they were more often transported in Mil Mi-8 helicopters, shown here. Mil Mi-8 helicopters carried 24 troops and were armed with rockets and antitank guided missiles.

Today's attack helicopters, also known as gunships, are armed with autocannons, machine guns, rockets, and antitank guided missiles. Their main purpose is to provide close air support for ground troops and destroy enemy armored vehicles, such as tanks.

The American AH-64 Apache was designed to take over from the AH-1 Cobra. The U.S. began using it in 1986. It has a 30 mm chain gun. It carries Hellfire antitank missiles on its wing pylons, as well as

Two Boeing AH-64D Apache Longbows fly low over an Iraqi T-62 main battle tank. They have just knocked it out during a battle in 2003.

70 general-purpose rockets. The unguided rockets pack a punch at 70 mm. During combat, Apaches could be heavily damaged and still continue their missions safely. The AH-64D Apache Longbow is equipped with a **radar** dome above the main rotor. It enables target detection while the helicopter is behind obstacles.

This Eurocopter Tiger of the German Army has a tandem seat that is used in most attack helicopters today.

Special forces use helicopters for attack, assault, and reconnaissance missions. The helicopters used by U.S. special forces are MH-47 Chinooks, A/MH-6 Little Birds, and MH-60 Black Hawks.

The Boeing A/MH-6 Little Bird is nicknamed "Killer Egg" because of its shape. It is based on a modified OH-6A (see pages 16–17). The MH-6 unarmed helicopter has outboard benches designed to carry up to three **commandos** on each side. The AH-6 gunship is similar.

A rocket-propelled grenade (RPG) fired by Somali **militants** narrowly misses a U.S. special forces Boeing AH-6 Little Bird gunship during the **Battle of Mogadishu** in 1993.

It has two M134 miniguns, which are six-barrel, rotary machine guns. It also has Hydra 70 rockets, fired from rocket pods on each side. These agile helicopters are often used alongside MH-60M Black Hawk helicopters from the U.S. Army's 160th Special Operations Aviation Regiment (Airborne).

The MH-60M Black Hawk is a special forces variant of the Sikorsky UH-60 Black Hawk. In 1993, Black Hawks were used in the assault on Mogadishu in Somalia. Two were shot down by RPGs.

Helicopters were first used in the military for search and rescue (SAR) and evacuating the wounded from the battlefield during WWII. Today's military search and rescue helicopters do many different jobs.

The HH-60H Ocean Hawk's primary role is conducting combat search and rescue and the **insertion** and **extraction** of special forces. The Ocean Hawk is based on the Sikorsky SH-60 Sea Hawk. The Sea Hawk is used for antisubmarine warfare, antiship warfare, ship and submarine

A Sikorsky HH-60H Ocean Hawk rescues a pilot from the Sea of Japan during a search and rescue exercise in 2017.

resupply, and medical evacuation. Sea Hawks are based on the U.S. Army UH-60 Black Hawk. Black Hawks can operate from aircraft carriers and other naval vessels such as frigates, destroyers, cruisers, fast combat support ships, and **amphibious** assault ships, as well as from land bases.

One of the earliest SAR helicopters used by the military was the Piasecki H-21, nicknamed "the flying banana." It was used for search and rescue in cold-weather operations. It was also used in several wars.

Antisubmarine Helicopters

Helicopters play a major role in protecting a fleet of warships from enemy submarines. Special **sonar** equipment for detecting and locating enemy submarines is an important element of antisubmarine warfare.

Naval helicopters, such as the Russian Kamov Ka-27, carry dipping sonar and **sonobuoys** to locate submarines. These helicopters normally work in pairs. Once a submarine has been detected, a variety of antisubmarine weapons can be used. These include a homing torpedo,which aims itself

26

A Kamov Ka-27 hovers above the sea, deploying a dipping sonar. It is searching for submarines in the Baltic Sea during a search and destroy exercise with the Russian Navy's missile battlecruiser, Pyotr Velikiy.

by listening for the sounds of its target. The Ka-27 uses two rotors that spin in opposite directions to give stability during flight. They allow it to hover in all weather conditions. Its squat shape and short rotors mean that it can operate from smaller decks than larger helicopters.

The Westland Lynx is a British multipurpose military helicopter. It is used by the Royal Navy for search and rescue and antisubmarine warfare. The Lynx can be armed with two torpedoes or with four Sea Skua missiles or two depth charges.

Unmanned, autonomous helicopters, or drone helicopters, are some of the newest military equipment. They provide reconnaissance, fire support, and precision targeting for ground forces. They also assist in antisubmarine and ship warfare.

The MQ-8 Fire Scout is used by the U.S. Navy and Army. The short, stubby wings allow the drone to carry a variety of weapons and special equipment called mission packages. Fire Scouts carry two four-packs of

A Northrop Grumman MQ-8 Fire Scout leaves the deck of a Littoral Combat Ship (LCS), the USS *Freedom*. It is shown on a surface warfare test while at sea.

70 mm rocket launchers to give fire support to ground forces. These drones are controlled by pilots at a secure base on land or on board a ship, but Fire Scouts can also be programmed to return to base and land automatically.

The Black Hornet Nano is an unmanned military micro helicopter used by the British Army in Afghanistan. It has three cameras. It is used to fly into enemy territory to take video and still images before returning to the operator.

Helicopter Specs

More information on the helicopters in this book

Avro Rota
Length: 19.8 feet (6 m)
Speed: 110 mph
(177 kph)
Crew: 1

Bell H-13 Sioux
Length: 31.5 feet (9.6 m)
Speed: 105 mph (169 kph)
Crew: 1

Flettner Fl 282
Length: 21.3 feet (6.5 m)
Speed: 93 mph
(149.6 kph)
Crew: 1

Bell UH-1 Iroquois
Length: 57 feet (17.4 m)
Speed: 135 mph (217 kph)
Crew: 1–4

Bell AH-1 Cobra
Length: 53.1 feet (16.2 m)
Speed: 171 mph (275 kph)
Crew: 2

Mil Mi-24
Length: 57.4 feet (17.5 m)
Speed: 208 mph (335 kph)
Crew: 3

Boeing CH-47 Chinook
Length: 98.4 feet (30 m)
Speed: 196 mph (315.4 kph)
Crew: 3

Boeing AH-64 Apache
Length: 58 feet (17.7 m)
Speed: 182 mph (293 kph)
Crew: 2

**Boeing AH-6
Little Bird**
Length: 32.6 feet (9.9 m)
Speed: 175 mph (282 kph)
Crew: 2

**Sikorsky HH-60
Ocean Hawk**
Length: 65 feet (19.8 m)
Speed: 168 mph
(270.3 kph)
Crew: 3–4

Kamov Ka-27
Length: 37 feet (11.3 m)
Speed: 168 mph
(270.3 kph)
Crew: 1–3

**Northrup Grumman
MQ-8 Fire Scout**
Length: 24 feet (7.3 m)
Speed: 132 mph (213 kph)
Crew: 0

Glossary

Allied Relating to the Allies, or the nations that fought against Nazi Germany and the Axis powers during World War II

amphibious Military operations by both land and naval forces against the same target

Battle of Britain (July 10–Oct. 31, 1940) A military campaign during World War II in which the British Royal Air Force (RAF) defended the United Kingdom from air attacks by Nazi Germany's airforce, the Luftwaffe

Battle of Mogadishu (October 3–4, 1993) A battle in Mogadishu, Somalia, between U.S. forces and Somali militia during the Somali Civil War where two UH-60 Black Hawk helicopters were shot down. A force that included MH-60L Black Hawks was sent to retrieve survivors.

close air support Integrated and coordinated air strikes that support ground troops

commandos Specially trained military units used for quick or surprise raids

depth charges Antisubmarine weapons that explode at a specific depth of water, destroying or disabling a submarine

extraction To pull someone out of a situation such as a battle

insertion To put someone in place

Iraq War (2003–2011) A war in Iraq that began with an invasion by a U.S.-led coalition to overthrow Iraq's leader Saddam Hussein

Korean War (1950–1953) A war between North Korea, supported by China and the Soviet Union, and South Korea, supported by the United States and the United Nations

MASH Mobile Army Surgical Hospitals operated by the U.S. Army during the Korean War. Also the name of a 1970s television show.

pannier Stretchers that were fitted outside of the cockpit of a helicopter to carry injured soldiers

radar A detection system that uses radio waves to determine the range, angle, or speed of objects such as planes

reconnaissance Exploration by military forces of an area to get information about the positions, numbers, and equipment of enemy forces

sonar A technique that uses sound to detect objects on or under the surface of the water

sonobuoy A floating device that is dropped into the ocean and that uses sonar to detect submarines, and radio to transmit the information

Soviet Referring to the Soviet Union (1922–1991), a former union of states in Eastern Europe and Asia

Soviet-Afghan War (1979–1989) A war in Afghanistan where the mujahideen rebel groups, backed by the United States and Saudi Arabia, fought the Soviet Union and the government of Afghanistan for control of the country

Vietnam War (1955–1975) A conflict between North Vietnam and its allies, China and the Soviet Union, and South Vietnam and its allies, the United States, South Korea, Australia, and the Philippines

World War II (1939–1945) An international conflict fought in Europe, Asia, and Africa, between the Axis powers, including Germany, Italy, and Japan, and the Allies, including the United Kingdom, France, Canada, Australia, and in 1941, the United States

Index